Rags

Story written by Alison Hawes

Illustrated by Katy Halford

Mum packs up the picnic stuff.

Ann puts Rags the doll in
her backpack.

Ann jumps from a rock.

Splash!

Rags lands in the wet sand.
Her pink dress is wet.

A scruffy dog picks up Rags.

It dashes off, then drops the doll.

A red crab
grabs Rags.

But a gull picks
up the crab!

The crab drops the doll.

Help!

Rags lands back in Ann's backpack!

Retell the story

Take turns retelling the story with your child.

10